Congressional Research Service

U.S. Natural Gas Exports:
New Opportunities, Uncertain Outcomes

Michael Ratner
Specialist in Energy Policy

Paul W. Parfomak
Specialist in Energy and Infrastructure Policy

Ian F. Fergusson
Specialist in International Trade and Finance

Linda Luther
Analyst in Environmental Policy

April 8, 2013

Congressional Research Service

7-5700

www.crs.gov

R42074

Summary

As estimates for the amount of U.S. natural gas resources have grown, so have the prospects of rising U.S. natural gas exports. The United States is expected to go from a net importer of natural gas to a net exporter by 2020. Projects to export liquefied natural gas (LNG) by tanker ship have been proposed—cumulatively accounting for about 12.5% of current U.S. natural gas production—and are at varying stages of regulatory approval. Projects require federal approval under Section 3 of the Natural Gas Act (15 U.S.C. §717b), with the U.S. Department of Energy's Office of Fossil Energy and the Federal Energy Regulatory Commission being the lead authorizing agencies. Pipeline exports, which accounted for 94% of all exports of U.S. produced natural gas in 2010, are also likely to rise.

What effect exporting natural gas will have on U.S. prices is the central question in the debate over whether to export. A significant rise in U.S. natural gas exports would likely put upwards pressure on domestic prices, but the magnitude of any rise is currently unclear. There are numerous factors that will affect prices: export volumes, economic growth, differences in local markets, and government regulations, among others. With today's natural gas prices relatively low compared to global prices and historically low for the United States, producers are looking for new markets for their natural gas. Producers contend that increased exports will not raise prices significantly as there is ample supply to meet domestic demand, and there will be the added benefits of increased revenues, trade, and jobs, and less flaring. Consumers of natural gas, who are being helped by the low prices, fear prices will rise if natural gas is exported.

Electric power generation represents potentially the greatest increase in natural gas consumption in the U.S. economy, primarily for environmental reasons. Natural gas emits much less carbon dioxide and other pollutants than coal when combusted. Other types of consumption are not likely to increase natural gas demand domestically for a long time. Use in the transportation sector to displace oil is likely to be small because expensive new infrastructure and technologies would be required. There is discussion of a possible revival of the U.S. petrochemicals sector, but the potential extent of a change is unclear.

Getting natural gas to markets where it can be consumed, whether domestically or internationally, may be the industry's biggest challenge. Infrastructure constraints, environmental regulations, and other factors will influence how the market adjusts to balance supply and demand.

Environmental groups are split regarding natural gas use, with some favoring increased use to curb emissions of certain pollutants, while others oppose expanded use of natural gas because it is not as clean as renewable forms of energy, such as wind or solar. The use of hydraulic fracturing to produce shale gas has also raised concerns among environmental groups particularly concerned with its possible impacts on water quality.

The possibility of a significant increase in U.S. natural gas exports will factor into ongoing debates on the economy, energy independence, climate change, and energy security. As the proposed projects continue to develop, policymakers are likely to receive more inquiries about these projects. Proposals to expedite and expand LNG exports have already been raised in the 113th Congress, including in S. 192 and H.R. 580. Two other bills, H.R. 1189 and H.R. 1191, would reform the DOE's process for determining the public interest regarding LNG exports and prohibit exports of natural gas produced on federal lands.

Contents

Figures

Tables

Appendixes

Contacts

Introduction: Things Have Changed

The United States has exported some amounts of natural gas for close to 100 years, but has generally imported more than it has exported (mostly from Canada).[1] Within the next five years, the United States may become a much larger exporter of natural gas, particularly liquefied natural gas (LNG), for the first time. Increased development of U.S. natural gas resources—primarily shale gas—along with low domestic prices in recent years and idle LNG infrastructure, have driven the change in the U.S. position. As recently as the mid-to-latter 2000s, the United States was projected to be a growing natural gas importer. However, imports have been declining since 2005, while exports have been climbing.

U.S. natural gas exports require federal approval pursuant to Section 3 of the Natural Gas Act (NGA) (15 U.S.C. §717b), with the U.S. Department of Energy's (DOE) Office of Fossil Energy and the Federal Energy Regulatory Commission (FERC) being the lead authorizing agencies. Historically, exports have been primarily via pipeline to Mexico and eastern Canada, but natural gas companies are now considering exporting greater quantities of U.S. LNG by tanker ship to a number of other countries. From 1969 to 2012, the United States has exported Alaskan LNG almost exclusively to Japan, but the volumes of those shipments have been relatively small and Alaska's natural gas market has been, and continues to be, isolated from the rest of the United States. The prospect of the United States supplying a global market with large quantities of LNG from the lower 48 states raises concerns in Congress, particularly about a potential rise in what U.S. consumers pay for natural gas and effects on the economy.[2]

Developers of natural gas export projects and natural gas producers argue that domestic gas prices will not rise much, or significantly, if U.S. natural gas exports increase because the United States has ample gas resources to meet domestic demand. Further, they argue there will be economic benefits such as increased employment and an improved trade balance. Other stakeholders disagree, fearing that such exports could cause domestic natural gas prices to rise thereby hurting the economy. Some environmental groups fear that increased exports will cause more shale gas production, which they are against. DOE has received the results of two studies it commissioned about the impact on domestic gas prices of exports and the effect on the U.S. economy. It is still evaluating the results of the studies and other criteria before it decides on any additional permits to export LNG to non-free-trade countries.

U.S. natural gas prices are lower than those in other international markets, partly because of the competitive nature of the U.S. market. Nevertheless, natural gas prices within the United States vary by regional market because of transportation limitations, access to supplies, and differences in demand. As new volumes of shale gas are developed, these supplies will seek markets where little or no natural gas production has existed in the past. Over time, the U.S. natural gas market will reconfigure itself to balance supply and demand regionally and nationally. But getting new natural gas supplies to market may be an ongoing challenge for the industry, whether within the

---

[1] CRS held a seminar on LNG exports on March 1, 2013, for congressional staff. The seminar video is available for staff on the CRS website, http://www.crs.gov/programs/Pages/RecordedEventDetail.aspx?PRODCODE−WRE00058.

[2] Exports of natural gas from Alaska are viewed differently as those resources are isolated from the rest of the U.S. market because natural gas prices in the lower 48 do not justify building the required infrastructure to transport natural gas via pipeline or as LNG. Additionally, there are not many, if any, Jones Act-compliant LNG tankers to transport natural gas to the market in the lower 48 states. In DOE's analysis of U.S. LNG exports, it has not factored LNG exports from Alaska into its analysis regarding impacts on the U.S. economy and domestic prices.

United States or abroad. Infrastructure constraints, such as the availability of pipelines, environmental regulations, and other regulatory requirements will play a part in how the natural gas market adjusts. Exports of natural gas either by pipeline or as LNG will be a factor as the market seeks balance, especially on a regional basis. Hence the potential export of more U.S. natural gas may have economic effects that vary significantly from region to region, and regional impacts may diverge from impacts on the nation as a whole.

Other issues have also been raised regarding natural gas exports. Environmental groups are divided on the desirability of greater use of natural gas at home and abroad. Advocates see it as reducing emissions compared to other hydrocarbons, whereas opponents point out that natural gas still emits carbon dioxide and other pollutants.⌐ Concerns about contamination of water supplies during gas production have been raised because of the use of hydraulic fracturing ("fracking"), the technique for extracting shale gas which uses water, sand, and chemicals to create fissures in shale, allowing the trapped natural gas to be cost-effectively extracted.[3] Other groups want to see greater use of natural gas in the U.S. economy for economic and national security concerns before it is exported overseas.[4]

The prospect of growing U.S. natural gas exports, particularly LNG, portends to be a factor as Congress debates the economy, energy independence, climate change, and energy security. Bills to expedite and expand LNG exports have already been introduced in the 113th Congress, including S. 192 and H.R. 580. Two other bills, H.R. 1189 and H.R. 1191, would reform the DOE's process for determining the public interest regarding LNG exports and prohibit exports of natural gas produced on federal lands. This report examines what has changed in the U.S. natural gas market and the prospects and implications of the United States becoming a significant net natural gas exporter.

Background: Natural Gas Exports Are Not New

Heading into the 2000s, the United States was expected to be a growing importer of natural gas because domestic production was declining and demand was rising (see **Figure 1**). The U.S. Energy Information Administration (EIA) in its 1999 Annual Energy Outlook forecasted that net natural gas imports would grow between 1997 and 2020 from 12.9% of consumption to 15.5%, based on consumption growing faster than production.[5] To accommodate the potential increase in imports, five new LNG import terminals were built by industry in the latter half of the 2000s and some existing facilities were re-commissioned and expanded. The United States currently has LNG import capacity of almost 14 billion cubic feet per day (bcf/d) or over five trillion cubic feet (tcf) per year. However, higher domestic production—mainly from shale gas development—has made imports unnecessary, leaving existing import capacity mostly idle. (See **Table B-1** for the U.S. supply and demand balance.) In its Annual Energy Outlook 2013 Early Release, EIA

---

[3] For additional information and analysis of shale gas and fracking see CRS Report R41760, *Hydraulic Fracturing and Safe Drinking Water Act Regulatory Issues*, by Mary Tiemann and Adam Vann.

[4] For additional information about natural gas and the U.S. economy see CRS Report R42814, *Natural Gas in the U.S. Economy: Opportunities for Growth* , by Robert Pirog and Michael Ratner.

[5] U.S. Energy Information Administration (EIA), *Annual Energy Outlook 1999 with Projections to 2020*, DOE/EIA-0383(99), Washington, DC, December 1998, p. 71, http://www.eia.gov/oiaf/archive/aeo99/pdf/0383(99).pdf.

projects that the United States will be a net LNG exporter by 2016 and a net natural gas exporter by 2020.[6]

The abundance of new domestic natural gas supplies shifted industry interest from building LNG import terminals to constructing LNG export terminals. As of March 7, 2013, there have been 25 applications for permits to construct liquefaction facilities at existing LNG import terminals (also known as regasification facilities) or for a new LNG export facility in order to export domestically produced natural gas as LNG. (See **Table 1**.) The total capacity is approximately 29.7 bcf/d. Additionally, seven companies have active permits and one other has been approved to re-export LNG cargos (take in foreign cargos, hold in storage, and then reload onto LNG tankers to go to foreign markets) from import terminals with three additional company applications pending. Increased pipeline exports to Canada[7] and Mexico may also rise if their domestic production continues to decline and their demand continues to increase.

Figure 1. U.S. Natural Gas Production, Consumption, and Trade
Historical and Projected Data

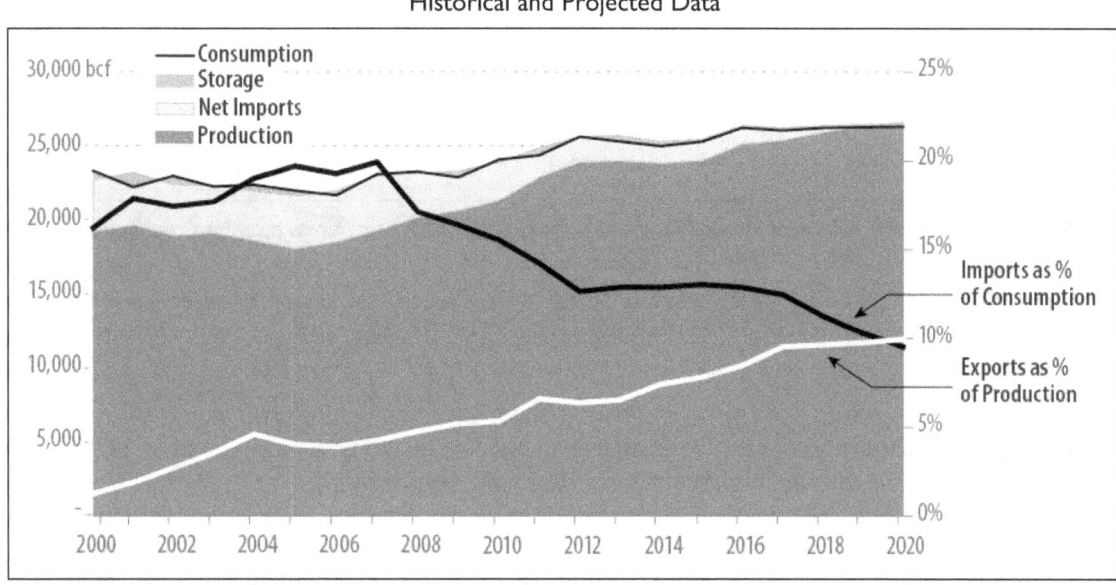

Source: EIA natural gas databases, http://www.eia.doe.gov/naturalgas/data.cfm, and EIA's Annual Energy Outlook 2013 Early Release, Natural Gas Section, reference case, http://www.eia.gov/oiaf/aeo/tablebrowser/.

Notes: Consumption equals Production, Net Imports, and Storage, but because of negative storage numbers for injection of natural gas into facilities the Consumption line in the graph does not exactly align with the sum of its parts. Exports of natural gas include the re-export of LNG cargos that comprise third-country natural gas supplies. Units are billion cubic feet (bcf) per year. Historical data are from 2011 and earlier.

Low U.S. natural gas prices relative to other international markets have spurred interest in exporting U.S. produced natural gas (see **Figure 2**). What effect exporting natural gas will have on U.S. prices and the overall U.S. economy are the central questions in the debate over whether to export. DOE commissioned two studies as part of its evaluation of whether LNG exports to

---

[6] U.S. Energy Information Administration, *Annual Energy Outlook 2013 Early Release*, DOE/EIA-0383ER(2013), Washington, DC, December 5, 2012, http://www.eia.gov/oiaf/aeo/tablebrowser/#release=AEO2013ER&subject=8-AEO2013ER&table=13-AEO2013ER&region=0-0&cases=early2013-d102312a.

[7] For additional information on the U.S.-Canada energy relationship see CRS Report R41875, *The U.S.-Canada Energy Relationship: Joined at the Well*, by Paul W. Parfomak and Michael Ratner.

---

non-free-trade-agreement (non-FTA) countries are in the public interest (see "DOE and the Public Interest Determination").

Figure 2. Select Global Natural Gas Prices

Nominal dollars

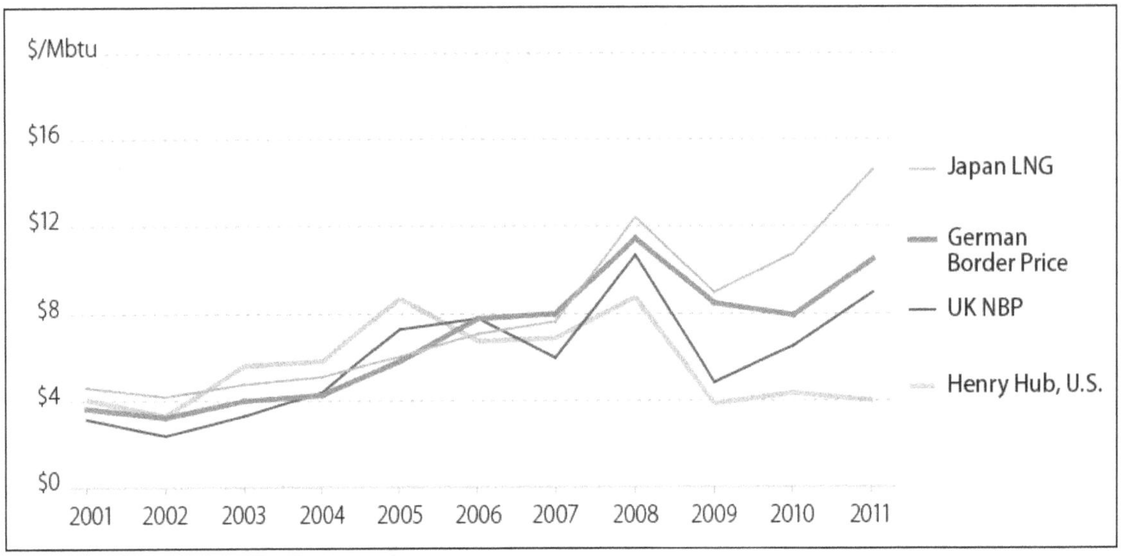

Source: BP Statistical Review of World Energy, 2012, June 2012, p. 27. http://www.bp.com/sectionbodycopy.do?categoryId=7500&contentId=7068481.

Notes: The German Border Price is a proxy for European oil indexed prices. Units = U.S. dollar per million British thermal units (MBtu). NBP is the market price in the United Kingdom referred to as the National Balancing Point.

The most recent EIA projections show the United States becoming a net LNG exporter in 2016 and an overall net natural gas exporter in 2020. The price projections, which extend to 2040, never reach the annual average high reached in 2008 (see **Figure 3**).

Lower natural gas prices since 2008 along with a large and growing resource base have prompted calls for greater use of natural gas in the U.S. fuel mix. This is one of the key arguments against exporting U.S. natural gas. Natural gas comprised about 28% of U.S. primary energy consumption last year and has averaged 24% per year since 1973. Instead of exporting U.S. natural gas, some say, the United States should increase use of natural gas in the electric power sector to displace coal, as an alternative transportation fuel to displace oil, and to provide fuel and feedstock to domestic industries such as petrochemicals. Some transition to natural gas is already occurring, particularly in the electric power sector.[8]

---

[8] For additional information about natural gas in electrical power generation, see CRS Report R42950, *Prospects for Coal in Electric Power and Industry*, by Richard J. Campbell, Peter Folger, and Phillip Brown.

Figure 3. Annual U.S. Natural Gas Prices, 1990-2040

Nominal dollars

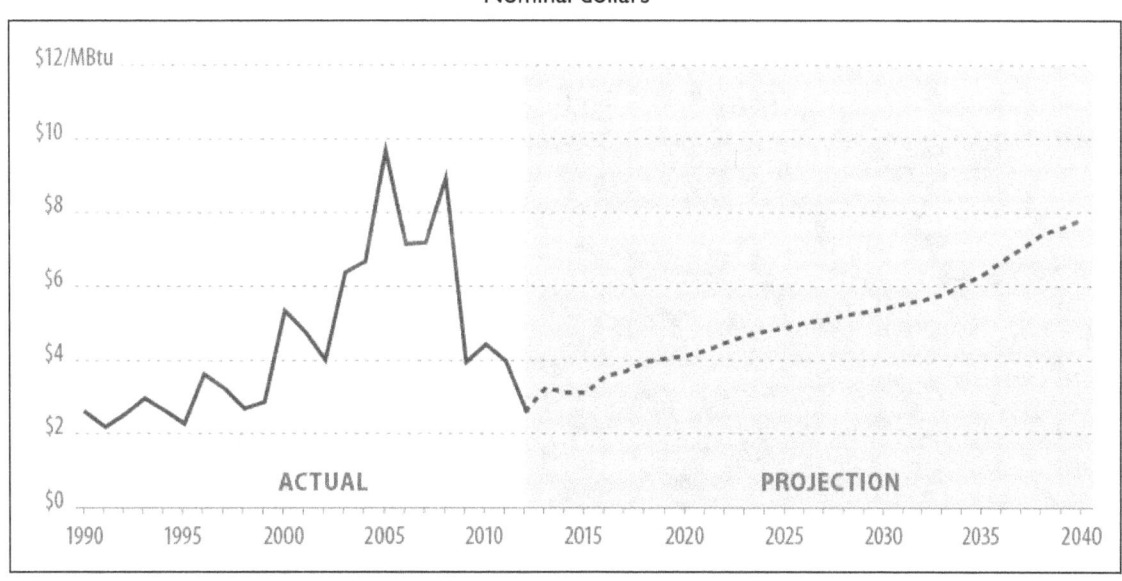

Source: EIA's natural gas price database, http://www.eia.gov/dnav/ng/hist/n9190us3a.htm and EIA's Annual Energy Outlook 2013 Early Release, Natural Gas Section, reference case, http://www.eia.gov/oiaf/aeo/tablebrowser/.

Notes: Prices reflect the average price at the wellhead in the lower 48. Projections are for 2011 forward. Units are dollars per thousand cubic feet ($/1,000 cu ft) in 2009 dollars.

U.S. Natural Gas Exports to Date

Total U.S. natural gas exports are currently relatively small but have grown since 1999, increasing nine-fold through 2011. The United States has been exporting natural gas since at least the 1930s, primarily to Canada and Mexico.[9] In 2011, 95% of exports were by pipeline to Canada and Mexico. Starting in 1969, a small amount of natural gas was also exported as LNG via the Kenai LNG terminal (Kenai LNG) in Nikiski, Alaska. Kenai LNG operated continuously from its opening until its idling in 2012, and remains the only LNG export facility in North America. Production of natural gas in the Cook Inlet of Alaska that supplies natural gas to Kenai LNG has declined too much to keep the facility operating.[10]

In 2010, the United States, through DOE's Office of Fossil Energy, allowed LNG import terminals to receive cargos of LNG, store the LNG, and to re-export the LNG to international markets. Seven companies have received permits to re-export LNG with four pending. This explains the "Other LNG" category that emerged in 2010 (see **Figure 4**). Prior to 2010, LNG exports had declined steadily since 2005. Growing U.S. natural gas production, primarily from shale gas, has decreased the demand for both pipeline imports and LNG imports, leaving the import terminals mostly idle. Additionally, eight of the import terminals have applied for licenses to construct liquefaction facilities to export domestically produced LNG, while there are 13

---

[9] Data are unavailable earlier than the 1930s and distinguished by country since the 1950s.

[10] The facility has not been dismantled, but is being maintained. It is possible that the facility could reopen if Alaskan natural gas production increases in the future.

applications for new liquefaction facilities, including floating facilities (see **Table 1**). In some cases companies that have partnered in a facility have both applied for licenses, but the volumes are only included once in DOE's data.

Figure 4. U.S. Natural Gas Exports
1980-2011

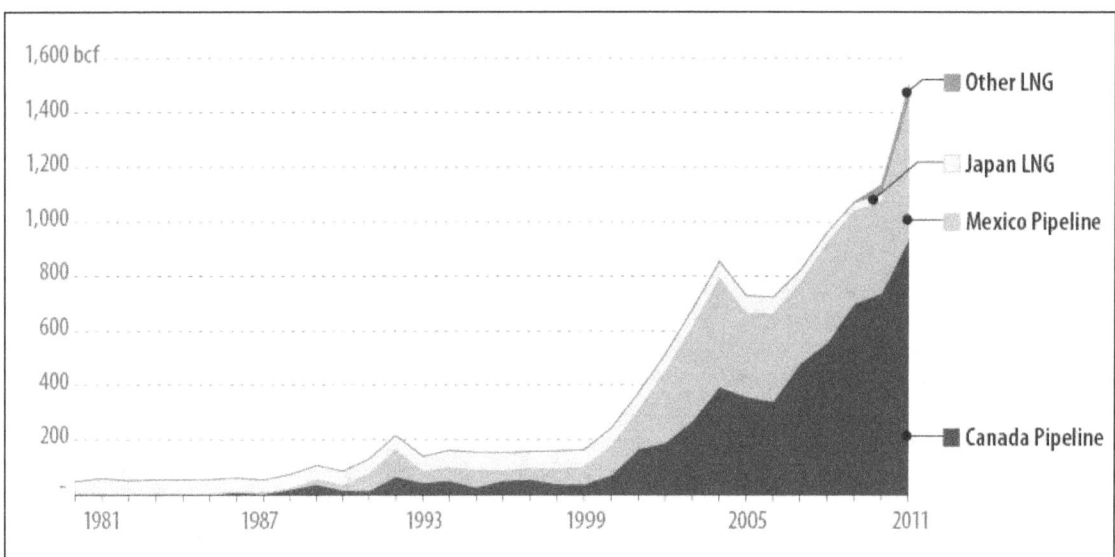

Source: EIA natural gas exports database, http://www.eia.doe.gov/dnav/ng/ng_move_expc_s1_a.htm.

Notes: LNG exports by volume are negligible to other countries besides Japan. Other LNG includes volumes that are re-exported from the United States after being imported from third countries. Units are billion cubic feet (bcf) per year.

Pipeline Exports Increase

Natural gas exports by pipeline have risen since 1999, increasing over 14 times through 2011 and accounting for about 95% of total natural gas exports last year. Canada and Mexico, both free trade partners, are the only recipients of U.S. natural gas exports by pipeline. As countries with which the United States has free trade agreements (FTAs), exports of natural gas to both are assumed to be in the national interest by statute, thereby expediting the approval process for projects. The St. Clair, MI, transit point to Canada and the Clint, TX, transit point to Mexico are the busiest for U.S. natural gas exports (see **Figure A-1**).

Gross exports to Canada and Mexico have both increased since 1999, growing 24-fold and 8-fold, respectively. Facilitated by the 1994 North American Free Trade Agreement, new cross border natural gas pipelines have expedited the trade. Canadian natural gas production has declined almost 15% since peaking in 2002, but still remains above the level of Canadian consumption. Some of Canada's imports of natural gas from the United States are from gas produced in Canada's western provinces, imported into the United States, and re-exported to Canada's eastern provinces. This is a cost-effective way to transport the natural gas given pipeline constraints within Canada. Mexican natural gas consumption has increased about 78% since 1999, growing more than production.

LNG Activity on the Move

U.S. LNG exports started in 1969 with the opening of the Kenai LNG export terminal in Nikiski, Alaska. Japan, the world's largest LNG importer in 2011, received almost 100% of U.S. LNG exports until recent years. The project has not been expanded from its inception and remains the only U.S. LNG export facility. From 2005 to 2010, exports from Kenai LNG declined almost 50% due to depletion of its natural gas supply. The facility is being maintained, but no gas is flowing through it.

LNG Re-Exports: The Latest Thing

Starting in 2010, DOE's Office of Fossil Energy, according to provisions in the Natural Gas Act, authorized LNG import terminals to receive LNG cargos from foreign countries and then re-export the LNG to other countries. Some LNG exporters try to take advantage of the idle U.S. import terminals and storage to wait for higher world prices. This trend almost doubled U.S. LNG exports to other countries, including new recipients Brazil, India, Spain, and the United Kingdom. This trend is likely to continue, particularly as natural gas prices in the United States remain lower than elsewhere and U.S. production remains adequate for domestic consumption. Using the facilities for re-export will help maintain their operating capabilities in light of this significantly decreased use to import LNG. Currently, seven companies have received permission to re-export LNG cargos from foreign countries with four applications pending.[11]

In order to re-export LNG, minimal or no additional equipment may need to be added to an import terminal. As mentioned above, DOE's Office of Fossil Energy must approve the change as does FERC.

Exports of Domestically Produced Natural Gas as LNG

There have been 25 applications for permits to export domestically produced natural gas as LNG, with a cumulative capacity of almost 10,836 billion cubic feet (bcf) per year or almost 50% of current U.S. production.[12] Eight of these liquefaction projects plan to adapt an existing LNG import terminal for export, which would require construction of liquefaction facilities at the import terminals, a major financial investment, with estimates ranging from $6 billion to $10 billion, mostly depending on capacity size. The other projects would construct new LNG export terminals, costing in the range of $20 billion. As of March 2013, almost all the projects have received approval to export to free trade countries, but only Cheniere Energy's Sabine Pass LNG project received DOE approval to export U.S. produced natural gas to non-free-trade countries.[13] Of the FTA countries, only Canada, Chile, Dominican Republic, Mexico, and South Korea have existing LNG import terminals, and South Korea is the second-largest importer of LNG globally.

---

[11] Department of Energy (DOE), Office of Fossil Energy, *Authorizations Database*, Washington, DC, November 8, 2012, http://fossil.energy.gov/programs/gasregulation/reports/LNG_Export_Auth Re Exports_11_8_12.pdf

[12] DOE, Office of Fossil Energy, *Authorizations Database*, Washington, DC, January 30, 2013, http://fossil.energy.gov/programs/gasregulation/reports/summary_lng_applications.pdf.

[13] Free Trade Agreement countries that require national treatment include Australia, Bahrain, Canada, Chile, Dominican Republic, El Salvador, Guatemala, Honduras, Jordan, Mexico, Morocco, Nicaragua, Oman, Peru, Singapore, and South Korea.

Table 1. Proposed North American LNG Export Projects

Company	Location	Volume (bcf/d)	Status DOE FTA/non-FTA	Status FERC	Status Under Construction
Sabine Pass Liquefaction	Louisiana	2.2	Approved/Approved	Approved	Approved
Freeport LNG Expansion and FLNG Liquefaction[a]	Texas	1.4 plus 1.4	Approved/Pending Approved/Pending	Pending	
Lake Charles Exports[b]	Louisiana	2.0	Approved/Pending	Pending	
Carib Energy[c]	Not Applicable	0.03 to FTA 0.01 to non-FTA	Approved/Pending		
Dominion Cove Point LNG	Maryland	1.0	Approved/Pending	Pending	
Jordan Cove Energy Project	Oregon	1.2 to FTA 0.8 to non-FTA	Approved/Pending	Pending	
Cameron LNG	Louisiana	1.7	Approved/Pending	Pending	
Gulf Coast LNG Export	Texas	2.8	Approved/Pending		
Gulf LNG Liquefaction	Mississippi	1.5	Approved/Pending		
LNG Development Company (Oregon LNG)	Oregon	1.25	Approved/Pending	Pending	
SB Power Solutions[c]	Not Applicable	0.07	Approved/NA		
Southern LNG Company	Georgia	0.5	Approved/Pending	Pending	
Excelerate Liquefaction Solutions	Texas	1.38	Approved/Pending	Pending	
Golden Pass Products	Texas	2.6	Approved/Pending		
Cheniere Marketing	Texas	2.1	Approved/Pending	Pending	
Main Pass Energy Hub[d]	Offshore Louisiana	3.22	Approved/NA	MARAD	
CE FLNG	Louisiana	1.07	Approved/Pending		
Waller LNG Services	Louisiana	0.16	Approved/NA		
Pangea LNG (North America) Holdings	Texas	1.09	Approved/Pending		
Magnolia LNG	Louisiana	0.54	Approved/NA	Pending	
Trunkline LNG Export[b]	Louisiana	2.0	Approved/Pending	Pending	
Gasfin Development USA	Louisiana	0.2	Approved/NA		
Freeport-McMoRan Energy[d]	Offshore Louisiana	3.22	Pending/Pending	MARAD	
Sabine Pass Liquefaction[e]	Louisiana	0.28	Pending/Pending		

Source: Department of Energy, Office of Fossil Energy, Natural Gas Regulatory Responsibilities databases, http://fossil.energy.gov/programs/gasregulation/reports/summary_lng_applications.pdf.

Notes:

a.   DOE received a new application from FLEX to add 1.4 bcf/d of capacity at the Freeport LNG terminal for both FTA and non-FTA countries.

b.   Lake Charles Exports and Trunkline LNG Export have both filed to export LNG from the Lake Charles Terminal. The 2.0 bcf/d volumes are not additive.

c.   Project will use cryogenic containers to export LNG in small amounts on cargo ships and does not need a specialized export terminal like the other projects.

d.   Main Pass Energy Hub, LLC (LCE) and Freeport McMoRan Energy LLC (FME) have both filed to export from the Main Pass Energy Hub. The 3.22 bcf/d volumes are not additive and only FME includes exports to non-FTA countries. As an offshore facility project, these companies have applied to the Maritime Administration (MARAD).

e.   This is an expansion of the Sabine Pass Liquefaction project at the top of the table.

Adding liquefaction capacity will require new equipment to be added to the existing import terminals. The modification or expansion of existing facilities, including liquefaction trains, storage tanks, compressors, piping, and other equipment, will require authorization from FERC. Depending on the nature of individual facility modifications, compliance with additional state or federal statutory or regulatory requirements may also be required. For example, facility modifications would be subject to some level of environmental review pursuant to the National Environmental Policy Act (NEPA). Potential regulatory requirements are discussed below (see "Authorizations to Export LNG").

Natural gas in Alaska is also attracting attention as a possible source for exports. The cost of producing and transporting Alaskan natural gas to the lower 48 for consumption is high when compared with current U.S. prices. As Alaskan oil production declines, companies may seek to monetize or sell their natural gas, which is typically re-injected into oil wells to boost production. There are also new potential natural gas supplies in Alaska that may be more conducive to export compared to North Slope natural gas. Potential Alaskan projects have not been included in the DOE-sponsored studies on exports as Alaska is considered an independent market from the lower 48.

Trade: Agreements or Disagreements?

Most companies seeking permits to export LNG have applied to export LNG to countries with which the United States does not have a free trade agreement (FTA) in addition to those with which the United States does have an FTA. As mentioned above, exports to FTA countries are presumptively considered "in the national interest" under the Natural Gas Act, as amended. All but one of those applications is pending with DOE. Of the 29.7 bcf/d of capacity applied for export by companies, 28.3 bcf/d or 95% is seeking or has received approval to export to non-FTA countries. As noted above, South Korea is the only major importer of LNG of the countries with which the United States has a free trade agreement. Of the other FTA countries, four have LNG import terminals, while the rest export natural gas, receive natural gas via pipeline, or do not import natural gas. In order for LNG export projects to be financially viable, they will likely need the ability to export to non-FTA countries.

The prospect of the United States limiting or restricting LNG exports has raised questions, particularly as a member of the World Trade Organization (WTO). The General Agreement on

Tariffs and Trade's (GATT) Article XI, General Prohibition Against Quantitative Restraints, states:

> No prohibition or restrictions other than duties, taxes or other charges made effective through quotas, import or export licenses or other measures, shall be instituted or maintained by any contracting party on the importation of any product of the territory of any other contracting party or on the exportation or sale for export of any product destined for the territory of any other contracting party.

There are exceptions to Article XI based on the conservation of exhaustible natural resources or the necessity to protect human health, which may apply if the United States restricts LNG exports.[14] However, these exceptions may be dependent on a country restricting its own production. Additionally, restricting LNG exports may put the United States in a contradictory position vis-à-vis cases it has brought to the WTO, specifically against China for limiting the export of rare earths and other metals. The position of the United States as a promoter of free trade may also be challenged.

Natural gas imports and exports comprise a small fraction of overall U.S. international trade, totaling about $22 billion in 2012, with about two-thirds of the value coming from imports.[15] The United States was a net importer of natural gas of almost $8 billion. LNG imports and exports accounted for 13% of the trade. Since 2000, the value of exports has averaged almost $2.5 billion per year while imports averaged over $20 billion.[16]

The Global LNG Market

If all the proposed U.S. LNG export projects were operational today, the United States would rank first in the world for global export capacity. However, U.S. LNG exports will face competition in the global LNG market. According to one study, global liquefaction capacity is projected to rise by almost 50% by 2020 (see **Figure 5**), including only one of the U.S. projects. Many non-U.S. projects are much further along than the U.S. projects. LNG trade was up over 10% year-on-year in 2011, accounting for 32% of all natural gas traded internationally.[17] Most LNG sold in the world is under long-term contracts, indexed to oil prices. The long-term contracts are needed to finance the liquefaction facilities, usually the most expensive part of the LNG supply chain, which includes LNG tankers, storage, and LNG import terminals. U.S. natural gas prices are market-based, which should give U.S. LNG export projects an advantage as the differential with oil-indexed-priced natural gas can be more than double the U.S. price (see **Figure 2**). U.S. LNG exports could add to the pressure for other countries to delink their natural gas exports—either as LNG or by pipeline—from oil-indexed prices. Japanese companies have been vocal about their interest in a natural gas-based pricing mechanism to reduce costs and exposure to oil prices. However, U.S. LNG export projects will still need to enter into long-term supply contracts, usually 20 to 30 years, to obtain financing, which may be a difficult hurdle to

---

[14] See GATT Article XX.

[15] U.S. Energy Information Administration, *U.S. Imports by Point of Entry and U.S. Exports by Point of Exit*, Washington, DC, January 31, 2013, http://www.eia.gov/naturalgas/data.cfm#imports.

[16] Bureau of Economic Analysis, Department of Commerce, *Trade in Goods databases*, June 14, 2010, http://www.bea.gov/agency/uguide1.htm#_1_19.

[17] *BP Statistical Review of World Energy 2012*, June 2012, p. 29.

overcome given existing market and financial conditions. Providing LNG to countries that use oil for heating, industrial processes, or electricity generation could also decrease demand for petroleum products, putting downward pressure on oil prices.

Figure 5. Actual and Projected LNG Production Capacity

2000 - 2020

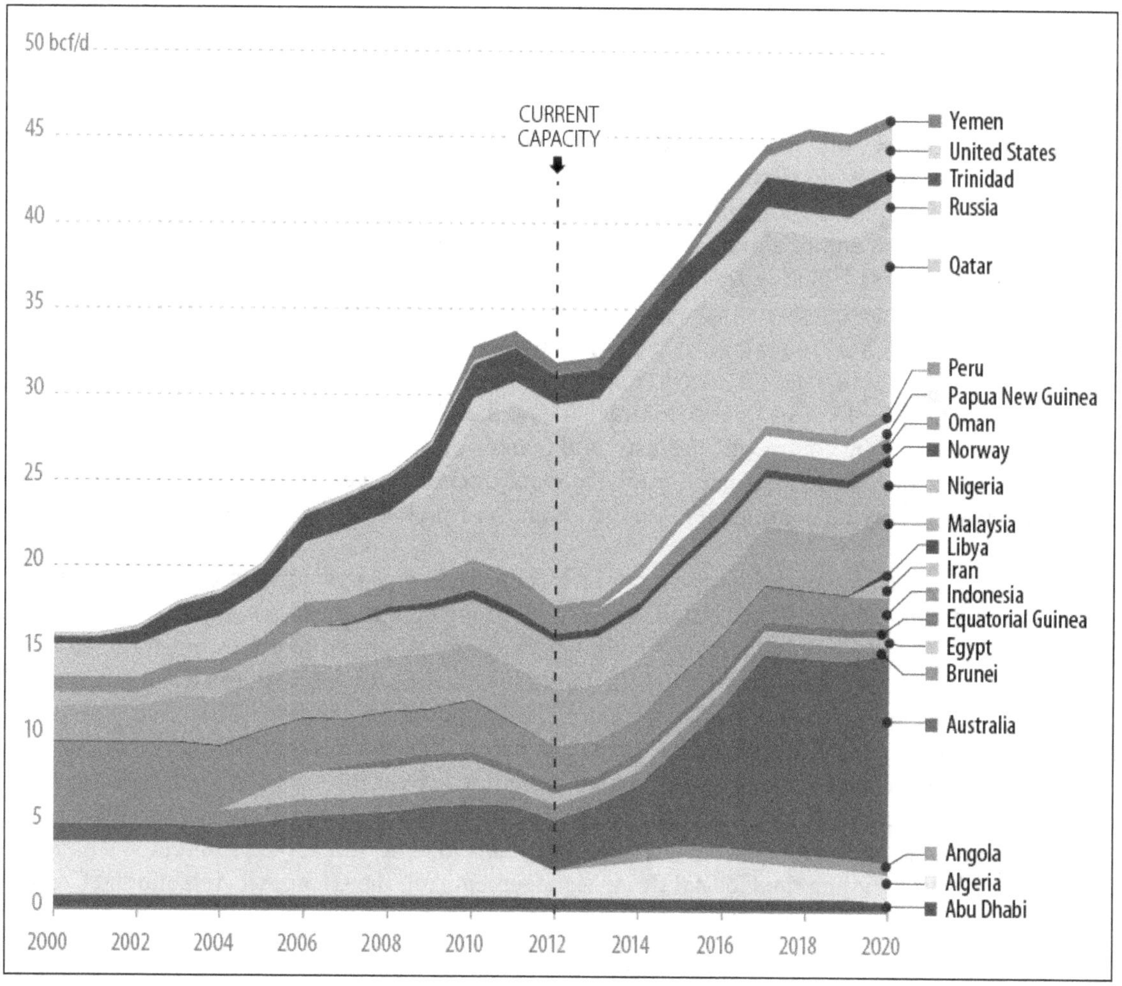

Source: PIRA Energy Group.

Notes: This graphic includes projects that are operating, under construction, or have reached a final investment decision. The only new U.S. project included is Cheniere's Sabine Pass terminal. The other proposed U.S. projects are considered speculative at this point. Units = billion cubic feet per day (bcf/d).

The dip in 2012 in **Figure 5** is due to major declines in Algeria, Trinidad & Tobago, Oman, and Indonesia. Algeria's two export terminals have been undergoing maintenance and one is being rebuilt. Trinidad & Tobago's decline is mostly because the United States is no longer a big importer of LNG. Egypt and Libya declined because of the turmoil in those countries.

Many of the projected projects in **Figure 5** are targeting the Asian LNG demand centers. Although the locations of most of the proposed U.S. export terminals are on the U.S. Gulf Coast and the East Coast, Asia may be the target market for U.S. LNG as it tends to pay higher prices for its natural gas imports. The widening of the Panama Canal, scheduled to be completed in 2015, would contribute to U.S. competitiveness in Asia. Europe has a lot of LNG import capacity and growing demand, but needs to continue to improve its infrastructure connections to transport gas to markets.[18] Russia, the main supplier of natural gas to Europe, may be put under increasing pressure by U.S. export projects to further delink its natural gas prices from oil. U.S. LNG exports could also provide options for some countries that are highly dependent on one supplier.

Authorizations to Export LNG

Pursuant to provisions included under Section 3 of the NGA (15 U.S.C. §717b), both the export of LNG and the construction or expansion of LNG terminals require authorization from DOE's Office of Fossil Energy and from the Federal Energy Regulatory Commission. With regard to exports, any person seeking authorization to export LNG from the United States, or to amend an existing import or export authorization, must file an application with DOE's Office of Fossil Energy.[19] Denial of an authorization is dependent upon the export being deemed "not consistent with the public interest." That is, there is a presumption that exports to non-FTA countries are in the public interest unless shown otherwise.[20] If the United States has an FTA in effect with the nation to which the LNG would be exported, that application will be automatically deemed consistent with the public interest.[21] LNG exports to non-FTA countries may also be authorized, but require the Office of Fossil Energy to publish a notice of the application in the *Federal Register* and seek public comments, protests, and notices of intervention as part of their public interest determination. DOE also can limit the amount of cumulative LNG exports, so each successive project may be contingent upon the volumes of previously approved projects.

Also under the NGA, any person proposing to site, construct, or operate facilities to be used for the export of natural gas from the United States to a foreign country or to amend an existing FERC authorization, including the modification of existing authorized facilities, must file an application for authorization with FERC.[22] In addition to FERC, the Department of Homeland Security's U.S. Coast Guard and the Department of Transportation's Office of Pipeline Safety (OPS), under the Pipeline and Hazardous Materials Safety Administration (PHMSA), may also be responsible for exercising some level of regulatory authority over the siting, design, construction, expansion, and operation of LNG facilities, and related land and marine safety and security issues. Projects related to LNG exports or LNG terminals may be subject to requirements under other federal law, including the Coastal Zone Management Act, the Clean Air Act, and the Clean Water Act.

---

[18] For more information on Europe's natural gas situation, see CRS Report R42405, *Europe's Energy Security: Options and Challenges to Natural Gas Supply Diversification*, coordinated by Michael Ratner.

[19] Requirements applicable to LNG exports are specified under Section 3 of the NGA (15 U.S.C. §717b). Regulations implementing requirements applicable to the export authorization application process were established under 10 C.F.R. Part 590, the "Administrative Procedures with Respect to the Import and Export of Natural Gas."

[20] Applicants seeking authorization to export LNG may seek either a blanket or a long-term authorization. The blanket authorization enables the applicant to export on a short-term or spot market basis for up to two years. The long-term authorization is used when an applicant has, or intends to have, a signed gas purchase or sales agreement/contract for a period of time longer than two years.

[21] See 15 U.S.C.§717b(c). Regulations implementing this section of the NGA were promulgated under 18 C.F.R. Part 153, "Applications for Authorization to Construct, Operate, or Modify Facilities Used for the Export or Import of Natural Gas."

[22] Pursuant to 15 U.S.C. §717b(e)(1).

Compliance with one environmental law applies to all DOE authorizations required under Section 3 of the NGA—the National Environmental Policy Act (NEPA, 42 U.S.C. 4321 *et seq.*). Pursuant to NEPA, DOE and other agencies are required to identify and document the environmental impacts of an action *before* a final agency decision is made. For projects related to LNG exports, the level of environmental review and documentation required will generally depend on whether the proposed action or project will require the construction of major new natural gas pipelines or related facilities or minor modifications of existing pipelines or related facilities.

DOE and the Public Interest Determination

As part of its process in determining whether LNG exports to non-FTA countries are "not consistent with the public interest," DOE's Office of Fossil Energy commissioned two studies: (1) a domestic price impact study by EIA and released in January 2012,[23] and (2) an economic impact study by NERA Economic Consulting (NERA) and released in December 2012. On February 25, 2013, DOE closed the comment period regarding the NERA study.[24] Almost 200,000 comments were received on the two DOE studies.[25] However, the results of these studies are only part of DOE's criteria for determining whether LNG exports to non-FTA countries are or are not in the public interest. In its approval of Cheniere Energy's non-FTA permit, DOE listed other criteria it used to make that determination: domestic need, adequacy of supply, the environment, geopolitics, and energy security. DOE has also provided insights into the "public interest" evaluation in a set of Policy Guidelines issued in 1984, Order No. 1471, and Delegation Order No. 0204-111. These were mostly to assess imports, but DOE has held that they also apply to exports.[26]

DOE has not laid out a timetable for when it will begin processing the pending applications or whether it needs additional information. The acting Assistant Secretary for Fossil Energy at DOE, Christopher Smith, declined to comment on a timetable for approving the non-FTA permits at a hearing before the House Oversight and Government Reform's Energy Policy, Health Care and Entitlements Subcommittee.[27] It has stated that it will begin "processing" the non-FTA applications according to:

1. All pending DOE applications where the applicant has received approval (either on or before December 5, 2012) from the FERC to use the FERC pre-filing process, in the order the DOE application was received,

2. Pending DOE applications in which the applicant did not receive approval (either on or before December 5, 2012) from FERC to use the FERC pre-filing process, in the order the DOE application was received,

---

[23] For the complete EIA report follow this link, http://www.fossil.energy.gov/programs/gasregulation/LNGStudy.html.

[24] For the complete NERA report follow this link, http://www.fossil.energy.gov/programs/gasregulation/reports/nera_lng_report.pdf.

[25] E-mail from DOE's Office of Fossil Energy, February 27, 2013.

[26] Department of Energy, Office of Fossil Energy, *Opinion and Order Conditionally Granting Long-Term Authorization to Export Liquefied Natural Gas from Sabine Pass LNG Terminal to Non-Free Trade Agreement Nations*, FE Docket No. 10-111-LNG, Washington, DC, May 20, 2011, pp. 28-29.

[27] U.S. Congress, House Oversight and Government Reform, Energy Policy, Health Care and Entitlements, *The Department of Energy's Strategy for Exporting Liquefied Natural Gas*, 113th Cong., 1st sess., March 19, 2013.

3. Future DOE applications, in the order the DOE applications are received.[28]

The December 5, 2012, date coincides with when the NERA study was publicly released. The basic conclusion of the NERA study was that LNG exports would benefit the overall U.S. economy. They acknowledged that there would be parts of the economy that would be hurt by LNG exports, mainly large consumers of natural gas, but that on a net basis the U.S. economy would be better off in all export cases. The net benefits would be highest if the United States could produce large quantities of low cost shale gas and that global demand for natural gas increases rapidly.

Both the NERA economic study and the EIA price analysis have been criticized. When EIA released its price analysis, the scenarios it examined per DOE's request were viewed as unrealistic. The high export scenario EIA examined was for 12 bcf/d, which is now well below the cumulative volumes for which companies have applied to DOE. According to EIA's analysis, the range of increases to domestic prices was 9.6% to 32.5%. Proponents of exports emphasized the former figure, while opponents focused on the latter. Both reports left enough latitude in their results for supporters and opponents of exports to promote their opinions.

The NERA report has attracted most of the attention in the 113th Congress, given the timing of its release. The NERA study, which used the EIA results, factored in international market parameters and macroeconomic impacts on the U.S. economy from increased LNG exports. In all the scenarios NERA examined, 63 in total, there were net economic gains to the United States, in spite of higher domestic natural gas prices, and the greater the exports the greater the benefits. The trade benefits from LNG exports outweighed the higher costs to the domestic economy. Criticism of the NERA report has focused on the narrowness of its results, the use of outdated data, and incomplete market information, among other things. Although the criticism may be justified, it is important to remember that the NERA study is just one part of DOE's analysis of determining which projects may be in the public interest. Similar to EIA, NERA was given a set of parameters to examine and asked for the impact on the overall U.S. economy. A full analysis of the NERA and EIA studies, as well as the myriad of other studies that have also been undertaken by other groups, is beyond the scope of this report.

Secretary of Energy Chu's announced resignation (pending confirmation of a new Secretary of Energy) adds another unknown to the DOE approval process. The Administration has nominated Ernest Moniz, a professor at the Massachusetts Institute of Technology.

Compliance with NEPA and Additional Environmental Laws

Both the Office of Fossil Energy's requirement to authorize LNG exports and FERC's obligation to authorize LNG terminal facility siting, construction, or expansion are considered federal actions subject to compliance with the National Environmental Policy Act. Broadly, NEPA requires federal agencies to identify and consider the environmental impacts of an action and to inform the public of those impacts before a final agency decision is made.[29]

---

[28] Office of Oil Gas Global Security Supply, *Pending Long-Term Applications to Export LNG to Non-FTA Countries - Listed in Order DOE Will Commence Processing*, Office of Fossil Energy, U.S. Department of Energy, Washington, DC, January 8, 2013, All pending DOE applications where the applicant has received approval (either on or before December 5, 2012) from the Federal Energy.

[29] Under Section 102 of NEPA, all federal agencies are required to include in "every recommendation or report on (continued...)

To ensure environmental impacts are indeed considered, before an authorization required under Section 3 of the NGA can be issued, DOE agencies must conduct the appropriate NEPA review. The level of documentation and analysis required for a given NEPA review will vary depending on the anticipated level of impacts of that project. Regulations implementing NEPA, promulgated by the Council in Environmental Quality (CEQ),[30] require federal agencies to—

- **Prepare an environmental impact statement (EIS)**—a full-scale review of the potential environmental impacts. An EIS is required when it is known that a proposed action will significantly affect the quality of the environment.

- **Prepare an environmental assessment (EA)**—a concise public document prepared when the significance of a proposed action is unclear. If it is determined that project impacts will be significant, an EIS must be prepared. Otherwise, a Finding of No Significant Impact (FONSI) may be issued.

- **Determine whether a Categorical Exclusion (CE) may be applied**—a category of actions that, based on agency experience, normally have no cumulatively significant impacts and, hence, are categorically excluded from the requirement to prepare an EIS or EA.

DOE supplemented the CEQ regulations to specify NEPA compliance requirements applicable to actions undertaken by its agencies.[31] Generally, the level of NEPA review required for authorizations related to LNG exports will depend on whether granting a request for authorization will result in the construction of major new natural gas pipelines or related facilities (such as siting and constructing a new LNG terminal) or a significant expansion and modification of existing pipelines or related facilities.

To date, the Office of Fossil Energy has determined that applications for authorizations to export LNG may be processed as categorical exclusions.[32] To make that determination, applicants must demonstrate that the project, among other requirements, will not violate applicable statutory, regulatory, or permit requirements for environment, safety, and health, or similar requirements of DOE or Executive Orders or involve extraordinary circumstances that may affect the significance of the environmental effects of the proposal.[33]

In regulations implementing NEPA applicable to FERC, DOE has identified the authorizations required under Section 3 of the NGA for the siting, construction, and operation of new LNG

(...continued)

proposals for legislation and other major Federal actions significantly affecting the quality of the human environment, a detailed statement by the responsible official on—the environmental impact of the proposed action" (42 U.S.C. §4332(2)(C)(i)).

[30] CEQ regulations, at 40 C.F.R. §§1500-1508, are broadly applicable to all federal agency actions.

[31] DOE promulgated "National Environmental Policy Act Implementing Procedures" at 10 C.F.R. Part 1021. Those procedures apply to all organizational elements of DOE, except FERC. "Regulations Implementing the National Environmental Policy Act," at 18 C.F.R. Part 380, apply specifically to FERC actions.

[32] See the U.S. Department of Energy's Office of Fossil Energy webpage "Natural Gas Import & Export Regulation, NEPA: Records of Categorical Exclusions," at http://fossil.energy.gov/programs/gasregulation/nepa_cx_determination.html.

[33] See the Office of Fossil Energy "Categorical Determination Form," issued February 6, 2013, for ENI USA Gas Marketing, LLC, application seeking authorization to export previously imported LNG from the Cameron LNG terminal in Cameron Parish, Louisiana, available at http://fossil.energy.gov/programs/gasregulation/cx_documents/Cat_Ex_12_161_LNG.pdf.

---

export facilities as actions that normally will require an EIS.[34] However, under certain conditions, FERC may first prepare an EA to determine whether an EIS is necessary. For example, for an application to authorize the modification of an existing LNG import terminal to allow for LNG export, FERC may prepare an EA and determine that the required modification will not result in significant environmental impacts. Such a determination might be made if, for example, the modification would require adding liquefaction and related equipment, but remain within the terminal's existing footprint.

To prepare the appropriate NEPA documentation for an LNG export-related authorization, the Office of Fossil Energy or FERC would be required to identify any other compliance requirements applicable to the authorization.[35] Applicable requirements may involve some level of input, analysis, or approval from another federal agency, or possibly a tribal or state agency. Following are selected federal statutes, including agencies that may have some jurisdiction over those requirements, that may apply to the construction of a new LNG export terminal or the expansion of an existing LNG import facility to include export operations:

- Clean Water Act—the U.S. Army Corps of Engineers, the Environmental Protection Agency (EPA), the U.S. Coast Guard, and state environmental protection agencies;

- Clean Air Act—EPA and state environmental protection agencies;

- Endangered Species Act—the Department of the Interior's U.S. Fish and Wildlife Service, the National Oceanic and Atmospheric Administration (NOAA) Fisheries Service, and state natural resource agencies;

- National Historic Preservation Act—the Advisory Council on Historic Preservation, the State Historic Preservation Officer, or Tribal Historic Preservation Officer; and

- Rivers and Harbors Act—the U.S. Coast Guard.

In addition to meeting appropriate environmental requirements, an authorized project may require compliance with additional safety or security-related requirements implemented by agencies including, but not limited to:

- The Department of Transportation's Office of Pipeline Safety (OPS) within the Pipeline and Hazardous Materials Safety Administration (PHMSA);

- National Fire Protection Association (NFPA); and

- Federal Emergency Management Agency (FEMA).

New Sources of Natural Gas: The Game Changer

The growth in U.S. natural gas resources, particularly from shale gas, and the projected continued growth are what make increased natural gas exports a possibility. U.S. natural gas reserves have

---

[34] See 18 C.F.R. §380.6(a)(1).

[35] For additional information on siting a liquefied natural gas terminal see CRS Report RL32205, *Liquefied Natural Gas (LNG) Import Terminals: Siting, Safety, and Regulation*, by Paul W. Parfomak and Adam Vann.

climbed 72% since 2000 and 49% since 2005. These data include reductions for natural gas extracted during the period and so are net increases. In recent years, the increase in reserves is mostly attributed to development of shale gas, which has grown from 10% of U.S. natural gas reserves in 2007 to 32% in 2010. By comparison, conventional U.S. natural gas reserves declined between 2007 and 2008, and fell again in 2010. Though the decline was marginal, it highlights the importance of shale gas to future U.S. natural gas production. Many industry analysts expect shale gas reserves to continue to rise and make up a greater portion of U.S. natural gas reserves unless new restrictions are placed on the industry, such as rules related to hydraulic fracturing, power plant emissions, etc.

In 2011, the United States produced and consumed more natural gas than it ever has—23 trillion cubic feet (tcf) and 24 tcf, respectively—while paying some of the lowest market prices for natural gas in the world.[36] The production figure of 23 tcf is of dry gas, which has been processed for consumption purposes, but the United States actually produced 28.5 tcf of raw natural gas in 2011. The United States is the world's leading producer of natural gas, surpassing Russia in 2009, and the world's leading consumer. After declining for the first half of the last decade, U.S. natural gas production rose 18% in the latter half, with shale gas accounting for 25% of production by 2010.[37]

Reserves and production data do not tell the whole story when looking at the U.S. transformation regarding natural gas supply. The term *reserves* has a specific industry definition that includes a technological component, an economic factor, and a probability of success among other criteria. To more fully understand the changes to the U.S. natural gas sector it is more appropriate to look at reserves and estimates for undiscovered, technically recoverable resources (UTRR) (see **Figure 6**). UTRR is an estimate of what can be extracted using current technology regardless of price. Using UTRR plus reserves, the United States has a natural gas resource base of 1,809 tcf or enough gas for approximately 79 years of production at 2011 levels. Compared with data from 2006, U.S. UTRR for natural gas has jumped almost 25%. Even this measure may not accurately reflect what will be extracted from the ground as technology is constantly changing. Just over the last few years, industry has been able to improve its shale gas extraction rate from about 5% to about 15%, thereby tripling what is recoverable.

---

[36] Many producing countries subsidize natural gas consumption, so their consumers do not pay a market price.

[37] 2010 is the latest year for which data are available for this metric.

Figure 6. Natural Gas Resources and Reserves

2006 vs. 2011

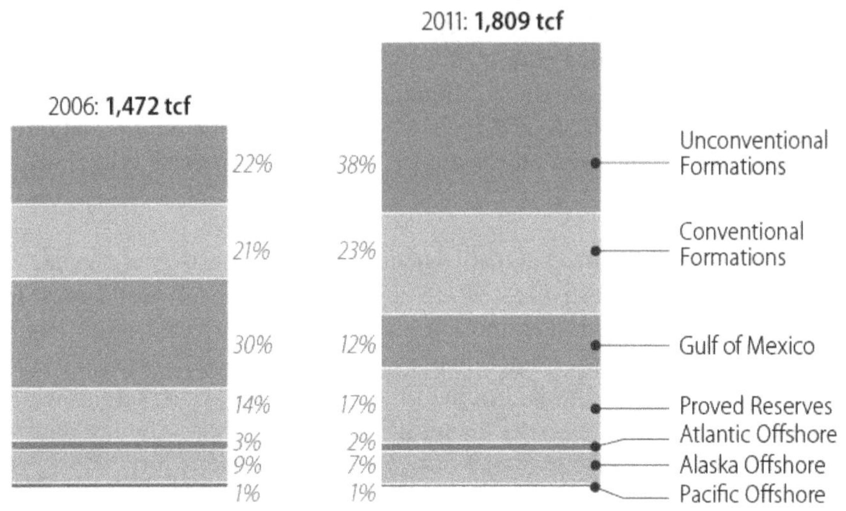

Source: Department of the Interior's U.S. Geological Survey and Bureau of Ocean Energy Management (BOEM) and U.S. Energy Information Administration.

Notes: The data for unconventional include some but not all of the shale basins, as some have not been assessed to date by the U.S. Geological Survey. Unconventional shales are fine grained, organic rich sedimentary rocks. The shales are both the source of and the reservoir for oil and natural gas, unlike conventional petroleum reservoirs. Undiscovered technically recoverable resources (UTRR) refers to amounts of natural gas estimated to exist by examining geologic characteristics of unexplored areas and recoverable using current technology. All the figures in the graphic above are UTRR except Proved Reserves, defined as a 90% probability of recovery using existing technology and at current prices. Units = trillion cubic feet (tcf).

Projected Future Growth

In 2011, natural gas was the most produced fuel, on an energy equivalent basis, in the United States, surpassing coal for the first time. This change was driven by the success of shale gas development. EIA, which makes projections based on current policy and information, estimated in its *Annual Energy Outlook 2013 Early Release* that overall U.S. natural gas production will grow 55% between 2010 and 2040. Shale gas will comprise over 50% of that production, up from 23% in 2010. During that time period, the United States is expected to go from a net importer of natural gas by pipeline and LNG to a net exporter by 2020, which is a change from EIA's *2011 Annual Energy Outlook* when there was no time period in which the United States was forecast to be a net exporter of natural gas. The United States is forecast to be a net LNG exporter by 2016, according to EIA.

Figure 7. Projected U.S. Natural Gas Production

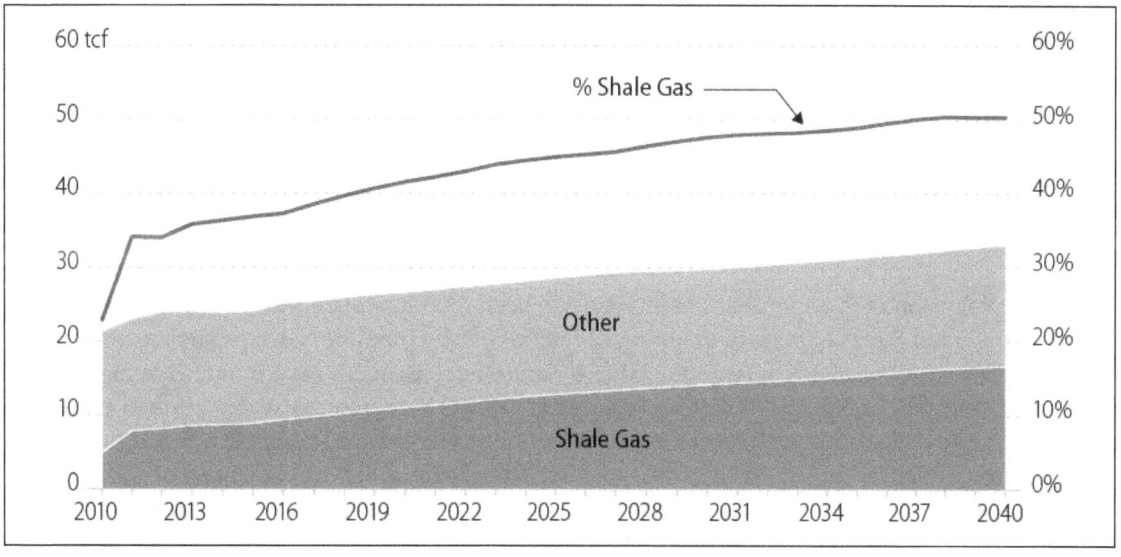

Source: EIA Annual Energy Outlook 2013 Early Release, Reference Case, http://www.eia.gov/oiaf/aeo/ tablebrowser/#release=AEO2013ER&subject=8-AEO2013ER&table=14-AEO2013ER&region=0-0&cases= early2013-d102312a.

Note: Units = trillion cubic feet (tcf) per year.

Natural Gas Liquids: A Production Driver

Natural gas liquids (NGLs) have taken on a new prominence as shale gas production has increased and prices have fallen. NGL is a general term for all liquid products separated from natural gas at a gas processing plant and includes ethane, propane, butane, and pentanes. When NGLs are present with methane, which is the primary component of natural gas, the natural gas is referred to as either "hot" or "wet" gas. Once the NGLs are removed from the methane the natural gas is referred to as "dry" gas, which is what most consumers use. Each NGL has its own market and its own value. As the price for dry gas has dropped because of the increase in supply and other reasons such as the warm winter of 2011, the natural gas industry has turned its attention to producing more wet gas in order to bolster the value it receives. Some companies have shifted their production portfolios to tight oil formations, such as the Bakken in North Dakota, to capitalize on the experience they gained in shale gas development. Historically, the individual NGL products have been priced against oil, except for ethane, and as oil prices have remained higher since 2005 relative to natural gas, it has driven an increase of wet gas production, thereby maintaining the amount of dry gas as a production "byproduct" despite its low price.

Congressional Actions and Considerations

There have been four bills introduced in the 113th Congress directly related to LNG exports, primarily to expand the list of countries that would get automatic approval beyond FTA countries. Other bills have been introduced that affect natural gas fundaments and infrastructure.

The Senate Energy and Natural Resources Committee conducted a hearing on natural gas, including exports, on February 12, 2013, and the House Oversight and Government Reform's Energy Policy, Health Care and Entitlements Subcommittee held a hearing on the DOE's permitting process on March 19, 2013. There may be additional hearings in the coming months. Some congressional representatives from the states where the LNG facilities are planned have submitted letters of support for the different projects to various regulatory agencies. Additionally, other Members have mentioned the possibility of natural gas exports in public statements, and some of those have expressed concerns about the potential effect on domestic prices, supplies, and the environment, among other issues.

Issues and Interests

The public focus on U.S. exports of natural gas has been on the applications to export LNG, despite the United States exporting much more natural gas by pipeline. Groups such as the Industrial Energy Consumers of America (IECA), a national association of manufacturing companies, and the American Public Gas Association (APGA), a national association of publicly-owned natural gas distribution systems, have filed motions to intervene against various projects.[38] Both of these organizations represent firms that use natural gas and would be negatively affected if natural gas prices rose. Natural gas producers and certain local businesses have supported the projects as they would benefit from access to new overseas markets and higher international prices. Analyses of the price effects of potential natural gas exports are underway and likely will receive greater attention as companies move forward with their projects. The Sierra Club has filed against projects on environmental grounds, particularly related to the source of natural gas for export.

Expectations about the economic impacts of greater U.S. natural gas exports depend on assumptions about the volume of exports, economic growth, market segmentation, and environmental regulations, among other market parameters. Some initial estimates project a modest rise in absolute terms in domestic natural gas prices if all the proposed export projects are built, premised on a relatively flat supply curve for natural gas. These estimates also project that U.S. natural gas prices will stay relatively low in historic terms as well as in comparison to global prices. Those in favor of exports add that increased production will result in increased revenue for local, state, and federal governments (through taxes, royalty payments, and economic development), more employment, an improved international trade balance, and reductions in natural gas flaring.[39] Natural gas consumers counter that higher natural gas prices abroad could eventually lead to higher prices in the United States, and possible supply shortages, as producers seek to maximize profits by diverting more and more U.S. natural gas to overseas markets.[40]

---

[38] Letter from Paul N. Cicio, President of Industrial Energy Consumers of America, to U.S. Department of Energy, Office of Fossil Energy, Office of Oil and Gas Global Security and Supply, December 13, 2011, http://www.ieca-us.com/documents/121310.pdf.

American Public Gas Association, "APGA Files Motion to Intervene and Protest Freeport Export Application," press release, March 28, 2011, http://www.apga.org/files/public/Press%20Releases/2011/Press%20Release%20-%20Motion%20to%20Intervene%20in%20Freeport%20Application,%202011.pdf.

American Public Gas Association, "APGA Files Motion to Intervene in Sabine Pass LNG Export Facility Application," press release, March 4, 2011, http://www.apga.org/files/public/Press%20Releases/2011/Press%20Release%20-%20Comments%20Sabine%20Pass-%20March%203,%202011.pdf.

[39] Flaring is combusting natural gas as a means to eliminate it because it may be impracticable to use, capture, or transport. Flaring is usually done as a safety or health precaution, during the exploration and development phases leading to production.

[40] Margaret Ryan, "USAEE Notebook: DOE Weighing LNG Export Price Effect," *AOL Energy*, Internet blog, October 10, 2011, http://energy.aol.com/2011/10/10/usaee-notebook-doe-weighing-lng-export-price-effect/.

In the near term, increased use of natural gas in the U.S. economy is limited, primarily to electric power generation.[41] Natural gas-fired electric power plants account for a significant and growing share of U.S. natural gas demand. Although coal remains the dominant fuel for U.S. electric power generation, environmental concerns regarding atmospheric emissions is limiting its use and prompting the retirement of older coal plants that are less equipped to curtail emissions. Switching from coal to natural gas in electric power generation may consume incremental U.S. natural gas supply increases before exports do. There are many proposed petrochemicals projects, but these are at various stages of development and will take a number of years to come to fruition. Other sectors such as transportation, industrial, commercial, and residential are not likely to see a substantial rise in natural gas demand in the next couple of years. This could change if technologies can be improved to increase the use of natural gas in transportation, such as gas-to-liquids, natural gas vehicles, or electric vehicles (assuming the electricity is generated by natural gas). Although proponents see strategic value in such fuel-switching as a means to reduce U.S. dependence on imported oil, high technology costs diminish this prospect in the near term.

Although much less attention is paid to natural gas exports by pipeline, it is possible that these will continue to increase as more shale gas is developed. Canada's natural gas production has been declining, but it is possible this will be reversed as Canada develops its own shale gas resources, which are estimated to be large. However, Canadian consumption may also increase as production from oil sands is projected to rise. Natural gas is heavily used in the extraction of petroleum from oil sands. Canada also has at least two of its own LNG export projects being considered. A recent EIA study estimated Canada's technically recoverable shale gas resources at 388 trillion cubic feet, almost 70 years' worth at the country's current production rate.[42] If Canada develops these resources, they could be an additional source of natural gas for the United States as well.

Mexico's natural gas production has been rising steadily for the last decade, but not quickly enough to keep up with consumption. Imports now account for over 26% of consumption compared to under 10% in 2000, and imports from the United States made up over three-quarters of all natural gas imports to Mexico in 2011.[43] Although Mexico may have even more technically recoverable shale gas resources than Canada, 681 trillion cubic feet or 385 years at their current production level, Mexico is much further behind in developing these resources,[44] and will likely remain dependent on U.S. supplies to meet growing demand.

Receiving permits to export natural gas by pipeline to Canada and Mexico is typically easier than receiving a permit to build an LNG export facility, even though pipeline projects require authorization from the Secretaries of Defense and State. Both Canada and Mexico are FTA countries and exports are assumed to be in the U.S. national interest by statute. Pipeline export projects tend to be less costly and easier to finance than LNG export projects may be; none of the latter have been built in the United States in 40 years.

---

[41] For additional information on natural gas in the U.S. economy, see CRS Report R42814, *Natural Gas in the U.S. Economy: Opportunities for Growth* , by Robert Pirog and Michael Ratner

[42] U.S. Energy Information Administration, *World Shale Gas Resources: An Initial Assessment of 14 Regions Outside the United States*, Washington, DC, April 2011, p. 4, http://www.eia.doe.gov.

[43] BP, *BP Statistical Review of World Energy 2012*, June 2012, pp. 23, 28, http://www.bp.com/sectionbodycopy.do?categoryId=7500&contentId=7068481.

[44] U.S. Energy Information Administration, *World Shale Gas Resources: An Initial Assessment of 14 Regions Outside the United States*, Washington, DC, April 2011, p. 4, http://www.eia.doe.gov.

As highlighted above, the development of shale gas resources will be a key factor in the United States becoming a net natural gas exporter. Infrastructure constraints within some of the major shale gas producing areas may limit the amount of natural gas that can reach markets and be available for export. Changes to the regulatory environment would also have an impact on natural gas production.

Environmental groups differ on the desirability of greater natural gas use in general. Although burning natural gas produces less pollution than burning other fossil fuels, it still emits greenhouse gases and other atmospheric pollutants. Some environmental groups view natural gas as a necessary bridge fuel to a zero carbon economy, while others want to go to the zero carbon economy directly. Some environmental groups see natural gas exports raising domestic natural gas prices, making renewables more viable. Additionally, there are concerns about risks to water supplies associated with hydraulic fracturing, the technique for extracting shale gas which uses water, sand, and chemicals to create fissures in shale, allowing the trapped natural gas to be cost-effectively extracted. The possibility of increased shale gas development and pipeline construction in the United States to supply overseas LNG buyers troubles some environmental advocates.

With natural gas prices low and projected to remain so, producers want new markets for their product. Exports represent one alternative outlet for natural gas.

Appendix A. Select U.S. Natural Gas Import and Export Infrastructure

Figure A-I. Select U.S. Natural Gas Import and Export Infrastructure

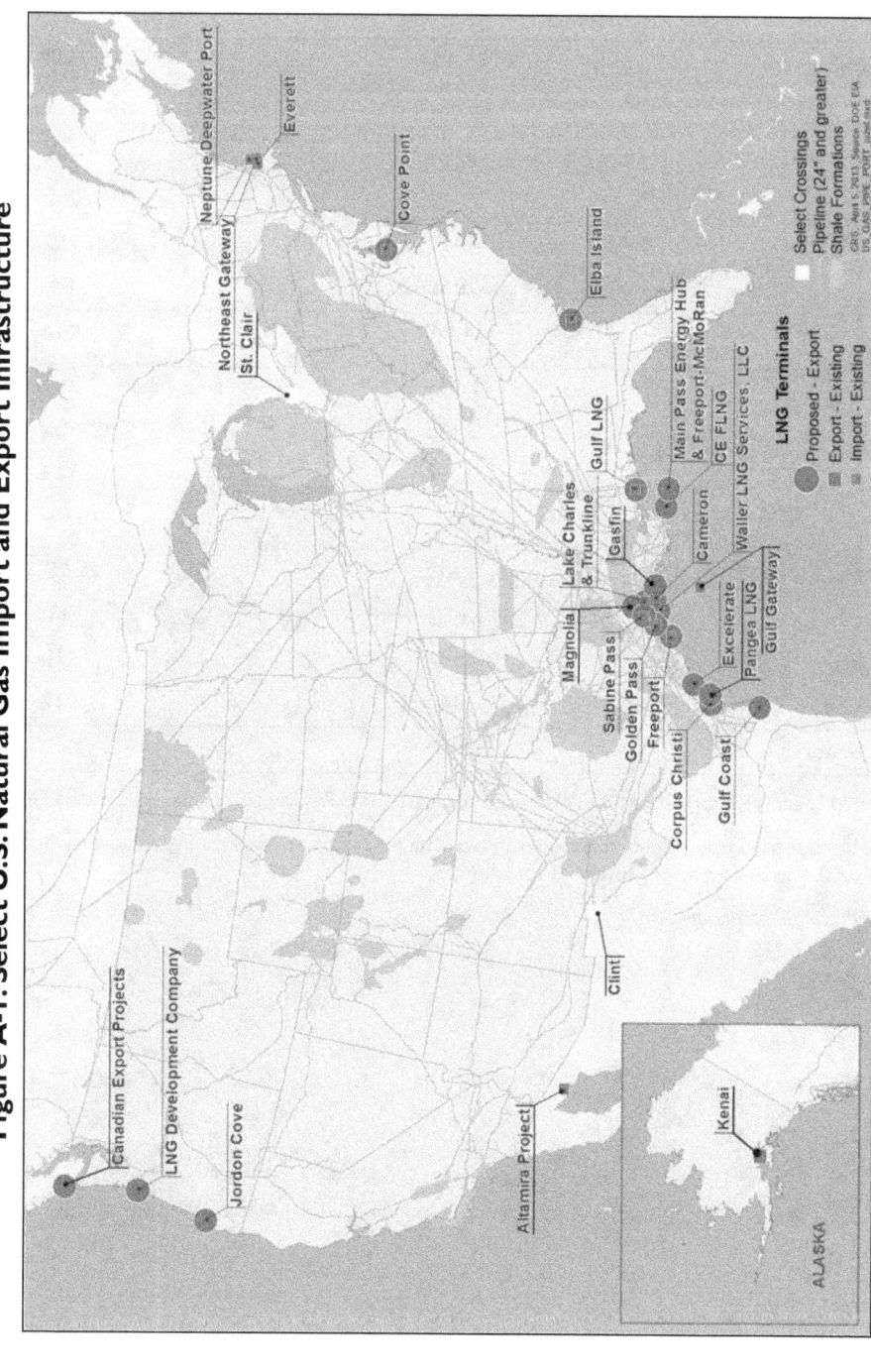

Source: Compiled by CRS from EIA sources.

Notes: Hawaii is not shown on this map because it has very limited natural gas infrastructure.

Appendix B. Supply/Demand Balance

Table B-1. 2012 U.S. Supply and Demand Balances

	Volume (bcf)	Percentage of Consumption
Consumption	**25,457**	100%
Commercial	2,905	11%
Electric Power	9,137	36%
Industrial	7,100	28%
Residential	4,177	16%
Other	2,138	8%
Productiona	**24,048**	**94%**
Net Imports	**1,516**	**6%**
Imports	3,135	12%
- Canada	2,960	12%
- LNG	175	1%
Exports	1,619	6%
- Canada	971	4%
- LNG (Alaska)	14	<1%
- Re-Export	14	<1%
Change in Inventories	107	**<1%**

Source: U.S. Energy Information Administration databases, http://www.eia.gov/naturalgas/data.cfm

Notes: Units = billion cubic feet (bcf). Table shows data for major sub-categories, which may not equal the section total, and sums may not total due to rounding.

a. Dry natural gas production.

Appendix C. Natural Gas Hub Map

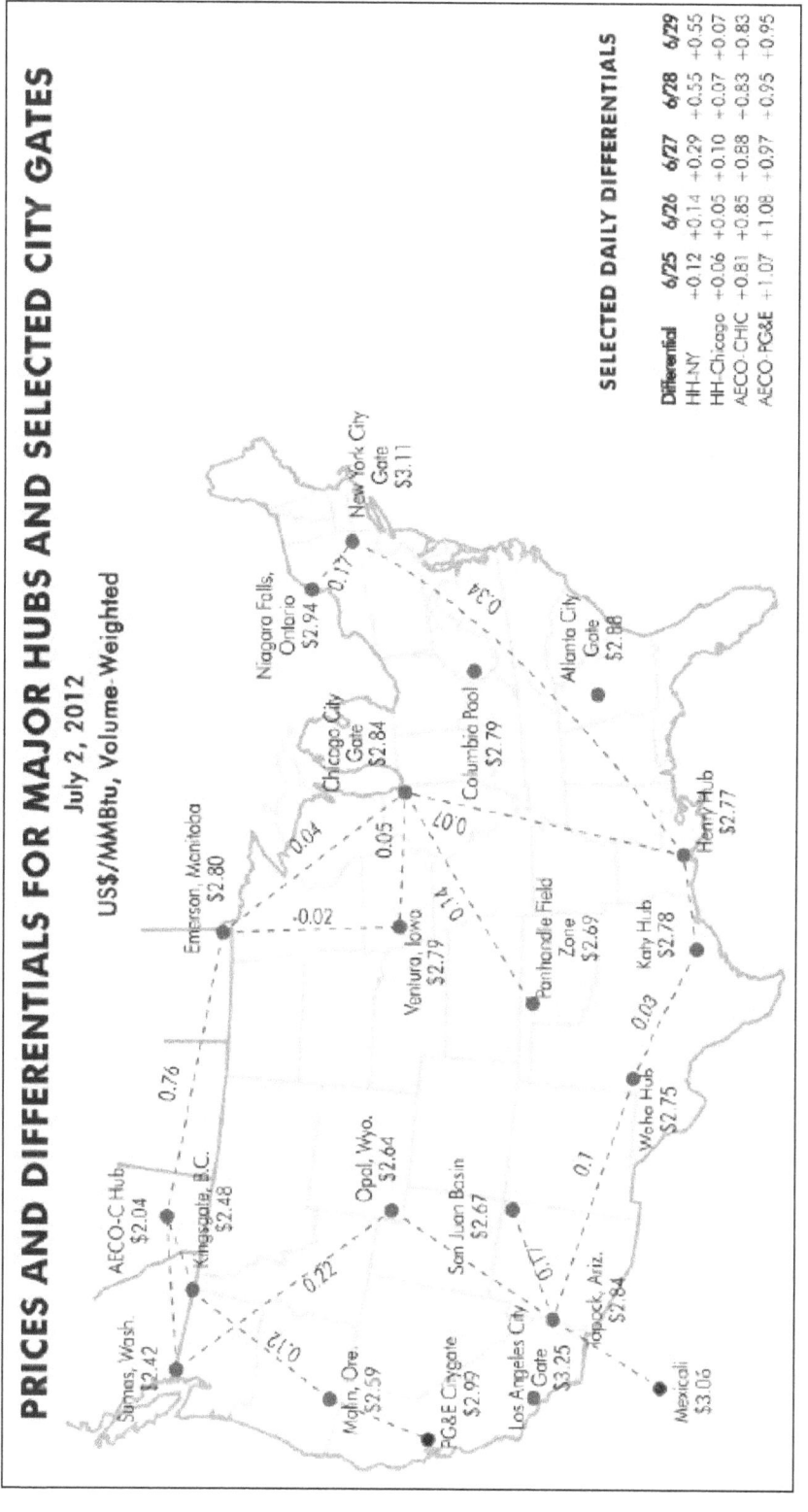

Figure C-1. Natural Gas Hub and City Gate Prices

Source: Natural Gas Week, July 2, 2012.

Notes: The figures along the dotted lines indicate transportation costs between hubs and city gates. Alaska and Hawaii are not included on this map as their markets are distinct from the lower 48 states.

Author Contact Information

Michael Ratner
Specialist in Energy Policy
mratner@crs.loc.gov, 7-9529

Paul W. Parfomak
Specialist in Energy and Infrastructure Policy
pparfomak@crs.loc.gov, 7-0030

Ian F. Fergusson
Specialist in International Trade and Finance
ifergusson@crs.loc.gov, 7-4997

Linda Luther
Analyst in Environmental Policy
lluther@crs.loc.gov, 7-6852

Acknowledgments

Elizabeth Roberts, Laura Hanson, and James Uzel of CRS's Knowledge Services Group contributed to the research for this report. Amber Wilhelm in CRS's Publishing and Editorial Resources Section contributed to the completion of this report.